Golf

— ❦ —

A Book of Quotations

Golf is like a love affair. If you don't take it seriously, it's no fun; if you do take it seriously, it breaks your heart.

Arnold Daly

A golf course is the epitome of all that is purely transitory in the universe, a space not to dwell in, but to get over as quickly as possible.

Jean Giraudoux

Golf is deceptively simple, endlessly complicated.
A child can play it well and a grown man can never
master it. It is almost a science, yet a puzzle
with no answer.

Arnold Palmer

I never pray on the golf course. Actually, the Lord answers my prayers everywhere except on the course.

Billy Graham

President Ford waits until he hits his first drive to know what course he's playing that day.
Bob Hope

When they start hitting back at me, it's time to quit.

Henry Ransom (when a shot rebounded from a cliff
and hit him in the stomach)

Golf is a fickle game, and must be wooed to be won.

Willy Park Jr

He's hit it fat. . . . It will probably be short. . . .
It just hit the front edge of the green. . . . It's got no
chance. . . . It's rolling but it will stop. . . . It's
rolling toward the cup. . . . Well, I'll be damned!

*Jimmy Demaret (commentating at the World Championship
in 1953 on Lew Worsham's winning wedge shot)*

My game is so bad I gotta hire three caddies –
one to walk the left rough, one for the right rough,
and one down the middle. And the one in the middle
doesn't have much to do.

Dave Hill

Golf is not like tennis, or basketball, or football,
where you can control your opponent. With golf you
cannot control your opponent.

Tom Kite

At my first Masters, I got the feeling that if I didn't
play well, I wouldn't go to heaven.
Dave Marr

A golf game doesn't end until the last putt drops.
Cary Middlecoff

I don't like doctors. They are like golfers. Every one has a different answer to your problem.

Severiano Ballesteros

There is one essential only in the golf swing,
the ball must be hit.
Sir Walter Simpson

When Nicklaus plays well he wins, when he plays badly he comes second. When he's playing terribly, he's third.

Johnny Miller

The entire handbook can be reduced to three rules. One: you do not touch your ball from the time you tee it up to the moment you pick it out of the hole. Two: don't bend over when you are in the rough. Three: when you are in the woods, keep clapping your hands.

Charles Price

I have found, in my own matches, that if you just keep throwing consistent, unvarying bogeys and double bogeys at your opponents, they will crack up sooner or later from the pressure.

Rex Lardner

Hole-in-One: An occurrence in which a ball is hit directly from the tee into the hole on a single shot by a golfer playing alone.

Henry Beard & Roy McKie

One reason golf is such an exasperating game is that a thing learned is so easily forgotten and we find ourselves struggling year after year with faults we had discovered and corrected time and time again.

Bobby Jones

Caddies are a breed of their own. If you shoot a 66, they'll say, 'Man, we shot a 66!' But go and shoot 77 and they'll say, 'Hell, he shot a 77!'

Lee Trevino

My golf swing is like ironing a shirt. You get one side smoothed out, turn it over and there is a big wrinkle on the other side. You iron that side, turn it over and there's another wrinkle.

Tom Watson

The vital thing about a hole is that it should either be more difficult than it looks or look more difficult than it is. It must never be what it looks.

Sir Walter Simpson

All games are silly, but golf, if you look at it
dispassionately, goes to extremes.
Peter Alliss

It's funny, but the more I practice,
the luckier I become.
Gary Player

What's over there? A nudist colony?

*Lee Trevino (after his 3 playing partners
drove into the woods)*

There are now more golf clubs in the world than Gideon Bibles, more golf balls than missionaries and, if every golfer in the world, male and female, were laid end to end, I for one would leave them there.

Michael Parkinson

Golf is a game in which a ball – one and a half inches in diameter – is placed on a ball – 8,000 miles in diameter. The object being to hit the small ball, but not the larger.

John Cunningham

If you watch a game, it's fun. If you play it, it's recreation. If you work at it, it's golf.

Bob Hope

A Scotsman is the only golfer not trying to hit the
ball out of sight.

Anon

All I have against it is that it takes you so far from
the clubhouse.

Eric Linklater

You hit the ball and if it doesn't go far enough you just hit it again, and if that doesn't work, you hit it again, and so on.

Robert Robinson

The difference between learning to play golf
and learning to drive a car is that in golf
you never hit anything.

Anon

As of this writing, there are approximately 2,450 reasons why a person hits a rotten shot, and more are being discovered every day.

Jay Cronley

I still swing the way I used to, but when I look up the
ball is going in a different direction.
Lee Trevino

When ground rules permit a golfer to improve his lie, he can either move his ball or change the story about his score.

Anon

There's only one thing wrong about Babe and me.
I hit like a girl and she hits like a man.
Bob Hope (referring to Babe Didrikson Zaharias)

It is a strange thing that we know just how to do a
thing at golf, and yet we cannot do it.

Bernard Darwin

Actually, the only time I ever took out a one-iron was to kill a tarantula. And I took a seven to do that.

Jim Murray

My goal this year is basically to find the fairways.

Lauri Peterson

Anytime a golfer hits a ball perfectly straight with a big club it is, in my view, a fluke.

Jack Nicklaus

Ah well. If we hit it perfect every day, everybody
else would quit.

Lee Trevino to Tom Watson

Most golfers prepare for disaster. A good golfer prepares for success.

Bob Toski

Suffering – ! I've got a hen back home in Charlotte
that can lay an egg further than that!

*Clayton Heafner (missing a 3 inch putt to lose the
Oakland Open by one shot)*

I'd like to see the fairways more narrow.
Then everybody would have to play from the rough,
not just me.

Severiano Ballesteros

I visualise hitting the ball as far as JoAnne Carner, putting like Amy Alcott, looking like Jan Stephenson and having Carol Mann's husband.

Dinah Shore

You've got to turn yourself into a material as soft as putty, and then just sort of slop the clubhead through. You'll hit much farther and with less effort.

Johnny Miller

If ah didn't have these ah'd hit it
twenty yards further.
Babe Didrikson Zaharias (referring to her breasts)

Golf is a good walk spoiled.
Mark Twain

The right way to play golf is to go up and hit the bloody thing.

George Duncan

Anytime you get the urge to golf, instead take 18 minutes and beat your head against a good solid wall! This is guaranteed to duplicate to a tee the physical and emotional beating you would have suffered playing a round of golf. If 18 minutes aren't enough, go for 27 or 36 – whatever feels right.

Mark Oman

Thou shalt not use profanity; thou shalt not covet thy neighbour's putter; thou shalt not steal thy neighbour's ball; thou shalt not bear false witness in the final tally.

Ground Rules: Clergyman's Golf Tournament, Grand Rapids

He quit playing when I started outdriving him.
JoAnne Carner (referring to her husband Don)

Real golfers tape The Masters so they can go
play themselves.

George W Roope

The only difference between an amateur and a pro is that we call a shot that goes left-to-right a fade and an amateur calls it a slice.

Peter Jacobsen

Everybody has two swings – a beautiful practice swing and a choked-up one with which they hit the ball. So it wouldn't do either of us a damned bit of good to look at your practice swing.

Ed Furgol

Golf is a game whose aim it to hit a very small ball
into an even smaller hole, with weapons singularly ill-
designed for the purpose.

Sir Winston Churchill

I don't think that was me that shot that eighty-four. It must have been somebody else. Actually, I was trying to get my handicap squared away.

Fuzzy Zoeller

I only hit the ball about 220 off the tee, but I can always find it.

Bonnie Lauer

Through years of experience I have found that air offers less resistance than dirt.

Jack Nicklaus explaining why he tees up the ball so high

Golf appeals to the idiot in us and the child . . . Just how childlike golf players become is proven by their frequent inability to count past five.

John Updike

I remember being upset once and telling my Dad I
wasn't following through right, and he replied,
'Nancy, it doesn't make any difference to a ball what
you do after you hit it.'

Nancy Lopez

Golf is a game in which you yell Fore, shoot six,
and write down five.

Paul Harvey

Wʰᵉⁿ he gets the ball into a tough place, that's when he's most relaxed. I think it's because he has so much experience at it.

Don Christopher (Jack Lemon's caddie)

Well, in plain old English, I'm driving it bad,
chipping bad, putting bad, and not scoring at all.
Other than that, and the fact I got up this morning,
I guess everything's okay.

Bob Wynn

When a putter is waiting his turn to hole-out a putt of one or two feet in length, on which the match hangs at the last hole, it is of vital importance that he think of nothing. At this supreme moment he ought studiously to fill his mind with vacancy. He must not even allow himself the consolation of religion.

Sir Walter Simpson

Keep on hitting it straight until the wee ball goes
in the hole.
James Braid

Players should pick up bomb and shell splinters from the fairways in order to save damage to the mowers.

British War Rule

Golf increases the blood pressure, ruins the disposition, spoils the digestion, induces neurasthenia, hurts the eyes, callouses the hands, ties kinks in the nervous system, debauches the morals, drives men to drink or homicide, breaks up the family, turns the

ductless glands into internal warts, corrodes the
pneumo-gastric nerve, breaks off the edges of the
vertebrae, induces spinal meningitis and progressive
mendacity, and starts angina pectoris.

Dr. A S Lamb

My caddie had the best answer to that – 'Just to let
the other one know it can be replaced.'
Larry Nelson explaining why he carried two putters

Confidence builds with successive putts.
The putter, then, is a club designed to hit the ball
partway to the hole.

Rex Lardner

My Handicap?: Woods and irons.

Chris Codiroli

If you drink, don't drive. Don't even put.

Dean Martin

Golf: a game where the ball always lies poorly and
the player well.
Readers Digest

It is good sportsmanship to not pick up lost golf balls
while they are still rolling.
Mark Twain

Over the years, I've studied habits of golfers. I know what to look for. Watch their eyes. Fear shows up when there is an enlargement of the pupils. Big pupils lead to big scores.

Sam Snead

If a ball comes to rest in dangerous proximity
to a hippopotamus or crocodile, another ball may be
dropped at a safe distance, no nearer the hole,
without penalty.

Local Rule: Nyanza Club, British East Africa
in the 1950s

I call my putter 'Sweet Charity' because it covers
such a multitude of sins from tee to green.
Billy Casper

Real golfers don't cry when they line up their fourth putt.

Karen Hurwitz

P ressure is going out there on the golf course
and thinking, 'If I don't do well, I'll have to rob
another bank.'

Rick Meissner (former touring pro & convicted bank robber)

He enjoys that perfect peace, that peace beyond all understanding, which comes at its maximum only to the man who has given up golf.

P G Wodehouse

You've just one problem. You stand too close to the
ball – after you've hit it.
Sam Snead (to a pupil)

At least he can't cheat on his score – because all you have to do is look back down the fairway and count the wounded.

Bob Hope

Never give up. If we give up in this game,
we'll give up on life. If you give up that first time,
it's easier to give up the second, third, and
fourth times.

Tom Watson

Always throw clubs ahead of you.
That way you don't have to waste energy going back
to pick them up.
Tommy Bolt

The little white ball won't move until you've hit it, and there's nothing you can do after it has gone.

Babe Didrikson Zaharias

The average expert player – if he is lucky – hits six, eight or ten real shots in a round. The rest are good misses.

Tommy Armour

It is nothing new or original to say that golf is played one stroke at a time. But it took me many years to realise it.

Bobby Jones

Sure, the purses are obscene. The average worker, let's say, makes $25,000 a year, while a golfer makes $25,000 for finishing 10th. Our values have departed somewhat.

Tom Watson (1989)

True golfers do not play the game as a form of stress management. Quite the reverse. They play to establish superiority over (a) themselves, (b) inanimate objects such as a small white ball with dimples in it, and (c) their friends. All of which can become rather tedious.

Colin Bowles

The nice thing about these [golf] books is that they usually cancel each other out. One book tells you to keep your eye on the ball; the next says not to bother. Personally, in the crowd I play with, a better idea is to keep your eye on your partner.

Jim Murray

The person I fear most in the last two rounds is myself.

Tom Watson (at the US Open)

I always keep a supply of stimulants handy in case I
see a snake, which I also keep handy.
W C Fields (putting whisky in his golf bag)

If you try to break the ball to pieces, the sod may fly farther than your shots. You've got to be gentle. Sweet-talk that ball. Make it your friend and it will stay with you a lot longer.

Sam Snead

W hat the nineteenth hole proves beyond a
shadow of a doubt is that the Scots invented the
game solely in order to sell their national beverage
in large quantities.

Milton Gross

Golf acts as a corrective against sinful pride.
I attribute the insane arrogance of the later Roman
emperors almost entirely to the fact that, never having
played golf, they never knew that strange chastening
humility which is engendered by a topped chip shot.

P G Wodehouse

Play is conducted at a snail's pace. Some golfers today remind me of kids walking to school and praying they'll be late. . . . Golfers used to check the grass of the greens; today they study the roots under each blade.

Jimmy Demaret (1954)

I've noticed some of them are off balance
when they swing. They're top-heavy. They've got
too much hair.

Ben Hogan on today's golfers (1970)

I was afraid to move my lips in front of TV.
The Commissioner probably would have fined me just
for what I was thinking.

Tom Weiskopf (on his 13 in the 1980 Masters)

Everyone gets wounded in a game of golf. The trick
is not to bleed.
Peter Dobereiner

Stroke play is a better test of golf, but match play is a better test of character.

Joe Carr

If you keep shooting par at them, they all crack up sooner or later.

Bobby Jones

A secret disbelief in the enemy's play is very useful for match play.

Sir Walter Simpson

A good player who is a great putter is a match for any golfer. A great hitter who cannot putt is a match for no one.

Ben Sayers

Fairway: A narrow strip of mown grass that separates two groups of golfers looking for lost balls in the rough.

Henry Beard & Roy McKie

The fundamental problem with golf is that every so often, no matter how lacking you may be in the essential virtues required of a steady player, the odds are that one day you will hit the ball straight, hard and out of sight. This is the essential frustration of this

excruciating sport. For when you've done it once,
you make the fundamental error of asking yourself
why you can't do it all the time. The answer to this
question is simple: the first time was a fluke.

Colin Bowles

The golfer has more enemies than any other athlete. He has 14 clubs in his bag, all of them different; 18 holes to play, all of them different, every week; and all around him are sand, trees, grass, water, wind and 143 other players. In addition, the game is fifty percent mental, so his biggest enemy is himself.

Dan Jenkins

No matter what happens – never give up a hole. . . .
In tossing in your cards after a bad beginning you also
undermine your whole game, because to quit between
tee and green is more habit-forming than drinking a
highball before breakfast.

Sam Snead

Golf is a typical capitalist lunacy of upper-class
Edwardian England.
George Bernard Shaw

The difference between golf and government is that
in golf you can't improve your lie.
George Deukmejian (Governor of California)

No man has mastered golf until he has realised that his good shots are accidents and his bad shots good exercise.

Eugene R Black

You get to know more of the character of a man in a round of golf than you can get to know in six months with only political experience.

David Lloyd George

Water creates a neurosis in golfers. The very
thought of this harmless fluid robs them of their
normal powers of rational thought, turns their legs to
jelly, and produces a palsy of the upper limbs.

Peter Dobereiner

If the tree is skinny, aim right at it. A peculiarity of golf is that what you aim at you generally miss, . . . the success of the shot depending mainly, of course, on your definition of 'skinny.'

Rex Lardner

Golf seems to be an arduous way to go for a walk.
I prefer to take the dogs out.

Princess Anne

The income tax has made liars out of more
Americans than golf.
Will Rogers

Golf is assuredly a mystifying game. It would seem
that if a person has hit a golf ball correctly a thousand
times, he should be able to duplicate the performance
at will. But this is certainly not the case.

Bobby Jones

Golf is not just exercise; it is an adventure, a romance . . . a Shakespeare play in which disaster and comedy are intertwined [and] you have to live with the consequences of each action.

Harold Segall

I play [golf] in the low 80s.
If it's any hotter than that, I won't play.

Joe E Lewis

Correct one fault at a time.
Concentrate on the one fault you want to overcome.
Sam Snead

The simpler I keep things, the better I play.
Nancy Lopez

Golf, like measles, should be caught young.

P G Wodehouse

Although golf was originally restricted to wealthy, overweight Protestants, today it's open to anybody who owns hideous clothing.

Dave Barry

They say 'practice makes perfect.'
Of course, it doesn't. For the vast majority of golfers
it merely consolidates imperfection.

Henry Longhurst

Love and putting are mysteries for the philosopher to solve.
Both subjects are beyond golfers.

Tommy Armour

If I had my way, no man guilty of golf would be eligible to any office of trust under the United States.

H L Mencken

Success depends almost entirely on how effectively you learn to manage the game's two ultimate adversaries: the course and yourself.

Jack Nicklaus

You hear that winning breeds winning.
But no – winners are bred from losing.
They learn that they don't like it.

Tom Watson

You must work very hard to become a natural golfer.

Gary Player

Golf is a day spent in a round of strenuous idleness.
William Wordsworth

I learn something new about the game almost
every time I step on the course.
Ben Hogan

I'll know I'm getting better at golf because
I'm hitting fewer spectators.
Gerald Ford

The uglier a man's legs are, the better he plays golf.
It's almost a law.
H G Wells

Go play golf. Go to the golf course. Hit the ball.
Find the ball. Repeat until the ball is in the hole.
Have fun. The end.

Chuck Hogan

Focus on remedies, not faults.
Jack Nicklaus

Golf is an ideal diversion but a ruinous disease.

B C Forbes

Reverse every natural instinct and do the opposite of what you are inclined to do, and you will probably come very close to having a perfect golf swing.

Ben Hogan

Looking up is the biggest alibi ever invented
to explain a terrible shot. By the time you look up,
you've already made the mistake.

Harvey Penick

Some people think they are concentrating
when they're merely worrying.
Bobby Jones

Golf is a game in which one endeavours to control
a ball with implements ill adapted for the purpose.
Woodrow Wilson

Don't play too much golf.
Two rounds a day are plenty.
Harry Vardon